THE TARGETED TRILOGY BOOK

BY DJ CHRIS

THREE BOOKS IN ONE:

THE COLD WAR NEXT DOOR

MY SYNTHETIC DREAMS

MY SYNTHETIC TELEPATHY

COPYRIGHT 2023

TARGETEDWEST EPUB/BOOK

Many people asked me for a hardcopy option of my targeted individual series, so here it is, thank you for the great support. I have talked to many people who suffer from the effects of the 4th industrial revolution of weapons for social and political control, they have shared similar stories as mine, so I **dedicate** this book to you, my reader or researcher. <u>You are not alone- no matter where you are on this planet</u>.

If you are one of the millions who suffer from this silent weapons abuse, then this collection is just for you. This is worldwide and a multi-trillion-dollar experiment that can be used for eugenics purposes to cull the unwanted humans and weaken earth through geo-engineering manipulation.

BOOK ONE OF THREE

THE COLD WAR NEXT DOOR BY TARGETEDWEST EPUB

COPYRIGHT 2019 TARGETEDWEST EPUB

Dedicated to the targeted individuals who suffer daily

TABLE OF CONTENTS

CB RADIO BUGABOO

It was a rainy day in the city of perps and felt like a good idea to ride my bike to the local radio shack to see if they have anything to interest me as kid, I was always very curious and radio shack filled that void for an only child kid of a freemason who was too busy to hang out with me. I finally got to the shack shop and saw a tube style radio In the as-is bin. It was discounted heavily.

Brought the rig home on my bike and plugged it in, with the antenna they sold me that day. It came to life with strange voices of people outside my helicopter mom's world of Mormon folks dropping by to shame us for not following the word of the ward, and my mom who watches TV all day and has no time for a curious kid with a million questions.

She had never finished school and had a limited vocabulary, except when it was time to put people down around her except me until I got older. She was a very big women over 6 foot like my father a local mailman who wanted to get rich at any cost, even if it meant neglecting his family.

It was a most catholic Spanish, Italian and Portuguese neighborhood, my mother prevented me from hanging out with anyone unless they are Mormon, so she forbids me to hang out with anyone she felt inferior to her false beliefs that made her isolated by her own devices. That CB Radio was my ticket to freedom, and I was going to use it to my best ability. I finally keyed up the old metal mic and spoke my first words on channel 23, one of the only ones that picked up since it was a crystal set

Bang bang bang on my window I heard a voice saying "you are breaking into my TV set" loud screaming at my bedroom window at 8 pm at night. My mother answered and it was the neighbor lady next door since her husband demanded her to summon us about his grand TV watching, his only passion.

Grumpy next door wouldn't talk to any-one, so he sends his wife a nice but strict woman from Lisbon who doesn't take crap from anyone. She said to me it is bothering her husband's TV and to knock it off. My mother didn't care for her and shewed he away. It was my birthday, and I talked my dad into getting me a fancy new 23 Channel CB Radio by telling him the interference next door would stop.

The new radio and antenna got my signal out to the area where I was able to meet many new friends but made the neighbors more upset. We hired a professional radio guy he added filters to their TV and my CB radio. It did not work. My father knew the radio was my only social network, since my mother was always sick, and did not drive. So, I carried on my radio talk and never worried since we heard nothing next door.

Then one day after school I come home to talk and see a green 1973 Plymouth fury wagon drive by slow with a passenger holding a stick and aiming at my antenna. Two men in suits drive by again and then park. My mother answers the door, and it is the FCC agents who drove 47 miles from their home office in San Francisco, CA to respond on several complaints from neighbors near my home. They measured my radio, and it was .4 too high on wattage and fined me. They also fined me for interfering with a television too. Mind you, I am a scared 15-year-old kid doing a very popular event in the 70's, the advent of CB Radio popularity and was not a bad kid. Convoy song about CB Radio played on the radio all day.

Grumpy next door was speed dialing the FCC often and was yelling at the employees at the agency, so they told me they had no choice. I moved my antenna to the garage and had my radio adjusted to be under the 5-watt limit. The perps next door quit talking to my family and me, they had the next-door guy involved too, so it was Co-Intel for a kid talking on a radio.

Few months later after getting the fine paperwork for the event and paying it, FCC decided to do a sweep of the entire area of CB Radio operators and they came back to my home again, since the whole citizens radio thing blew up, thanks to movies like Cannon Ball Run and more. Same routine, they measure my radio, and it is fine, but they still said the neighbors have been calling and yelling again, so they fine me again for bothering TV's. Two perp men from next door would bang and swear at me through my bedroom window often over the TV while I was a kid. They had no shame, because the TV was brain washing them into an altered state and they are too poorly educated to understand.

Grumpy was the manager at the fruit depo and couldn't talk well, he just yelled. Before Silly-Con Valley took over the entire Bay Area was orchards growing food and that was his gig, his wife canned fruit at the factory near-by. I turned 16 and was able to drive and set my dad's huge Chrysler up with a CB Radio and antenna system, so I escaped the perps in my hood. I joined a radio club, and we did a game called fox hunting which we triangulated each other like the FCC did with me instead using a loop antenna, that was directional.

As a kid, I never understood how people could be so glued to that crap TV set. But it was the only entertainment people had who were limited in mind. I'd ride my bike around the hood at night and see the lights of the TV in peoples window, it was a show of class for the middle class back then. One of the folks I met on CB told me that it is possible to mind control people, since he was an engineer for the Telstar satellite system recently launched. He told me the TV can brain wash too, so I understood why everyone got violent acting on my street.

SILENT TREATMENT

They, the perps next door managed to bad mouth me and give me attitude for years while I was a young adult, working 60 hours a week at my father business, and going to school full time. Calling the police when I parked my car the wrong way and other harassment tactics and not even waving. I would still use my bedroom radio at home, but way less since I was mobile and had a car with a unit installed.

We did not keep up with our yard because it was so uncomfortable to be watched non-stop by the elderly women across the street who bobbed and weaved when I waved at her in her kitchen window. So, they started addressing the yard often, and making complaints. One of the perps would fist fight with his daughter's ex hubby out front, so my mother told me to stay on the other side of the street. His wife claimed she can hear me on her electric stove coil, which is not uncommon.

She claims she had a nervous breakdown because of my radio, and treated me like crap for decades, she was a very poor actor when she was near me. Her real reason she broke down was her daughter was getting a divorce and the grandkids had to move in. Her husband may have come by and cut all my radio wires coming out of my bedroom window, after one of my CB radio sessions, I had left and came back in my car. It was raining heavy, so I went back to radio shack and got connectors and fixed my wires in one hour.

I took my work money and bought a used 1979 Dodge Magnum and put in a new cobra radio that was modified to have over 200 channels. I ran a 250-watt linear amplifier and could skip trace signals to countries like Scotland. I had the first digital police scanner mounted on the floor while I cruise with other hobby cars like mine on the main drag in town, The El Camino Real. I had gone rouge and I was not going to be pushed down any longer, little did I know that I was living in the best years of my life now that I escaped the Cold War Next Door.

The never-ending war that went on and on was over for now. The next generation of the perps the grandmother warned me about moved in next door and restarted the feud. The grandkids started calling the police often and other debauchery over legal medical cannabis smoke that I needed, in a single-family home not very close to them. The grandmother would puff cigarettes and would smoke me out of my patio often. I did not care as we were on a friendly basis again.

The once all elderly folks on my street died and renters came in to replace them. One renter, a reinstated lawyer worked for the DA and was an important AA member as he told me he was recovering. Old and young partied on my street and he did not like it. It was middle class parties not some dark drug event. He took a keen interest in me, since I told him I was sober and quit drugs many years ago. He argued cannabis was a drug and begged me to quit, even with my immune disorder diagnosis.

FULL ZERSETZUNG NEXT DOOR AND REMOTELY

It was 7am and the city decided to replace a section of the street in front of me. They always do a great job since the city is well managed and kept clean and in good repair. The day before September 10th, 2001, was bizarre as the news reported that a certain top person in the government said money was missing from the pentagon, and it was a matter of life and death.

Our friend called and said to turn on the TV, the towers are falling, the towers are falling like Tattoo on Fantasy Island when the plane lands. We turned on CNN and watched the event unfold. I told the workers out front on my street and they left in a hurry, leaving a shallow hole for a few days. The falling towers gave me PTSD, which I knew very little of since the Internet was in its infancy.

Our cannabis source was shady and had an agenda of his own and decided to sprinkle drugs on my purchase from him. I started not being able to sleep, realized this feels like the drugs I had experimented with in the 80's like many others did back in the say no to drugs decade. I confronted him and he told me he did. Between the PTSD and the drug, I asked for more.

The AA guy was watching my home and used his contacts at the local DA to get the sheriff to do a live Co-Intel event keystone cop style. For two weeks I was high as a kite and staying up at night. This gigantic storm showed up one night, in January of 2002, and it was the perfect time to scare the living heck out of me, using Air Theatre©. 4am, I hear a helicopter near-by, which was not true, it was above my roof.

We came outside and waved at them. It was a black EC-120 Euro-Copter used by the sheriff, the letters were so dark they cannot be seen at night. They had one man standing on the landing gear holding a device that looks like one of those old degaussing wands the old tv repairmen would use to make your TV look better. They flew off fast and never came back. I found the exact ghetto helicopter on YouTube years later.

The next day I can tell someone is watching me while high. I hid in the hallway and closed al the doors and sat on the floor. I hear a voice come out of my ceiling saying, "hey what are you doing in the hallway?". The Telstar guy told me about this years ago during a CB radio meeting so, I did not panic. They had me lay in my bed and I could not move for a day while they remote interrogated me.

They tried to get all my secrets which were few and boring, so I made up things while I was high. They covered everything, and asked over and over on questions, expecting a difference answer. The drug had a truth serum effect as I later learned street drugs were used for getting information out of suspects. I saw holograms that made me trip out and try to call the police to tell them I can see their police car out-front. The voices wouldn't stop so I flushed the rest of the small baggy and that was it no more drugs, because it gave me the losing hand, and I cannot defend myself if I am not sober.

I have talked to many folks on conference calls who had the drug thing turn sideways with the authorities involved or the V2K. The Patriot Act has a DEA parallel program, and I was a domestic terrorist over that small baggy and a party. I went to the AA guy to get a meeting list and started going to AA meetings which helps people with drugs too. I knew he may be involved but at that time I needed to be sober and going to meetings often, which I am sure I was followed.

I bought my first sober gift, a new 2002 Crown Vic. The same as the police cars but way nicer. AA guy tripped out and thought it was a Lincoln. Any time I had friends over AA guy would call me to make sure I am not doing drugs. He said I needed therapy, so he sent me to a cheesy drug place which charged 65 a week cash. The counselor was very verbally abusive. He had one arm, so I called him the one-armed bandit behind his back and quit. For less money, I found a real doctor who helped me find out the root of why I was doing drugs.

I told her that half of me thinks I need medical help and the other me thinks it is electronic. She said it was organic from drug use. After 18 years with her, she understands it can be electronic or spiritual, or organic. I still have no idea why I have synthetic telepathy or voices that I talk to like CB Radio. There are very few doctors that can help with mental issues and targeting, that is why this country and others have issues with violence.

I started a diary in 2003 and wrote a page often. I used the paper diary, to prevent erasure or hacking. I have several memoirs of my synthetic telepathy conversations, and a running narrative of my choice of drugs to stop the voices. The drugs did not help. The antidepressant did help me handle remote torture and having a new stress, my father getting dementia. He had the voices too; he was a Master Mason. We took care of him at my house which kept me busy and avoiding the ugly messages in my head.

My drugged-out stepsister called one day and said my father had long term care insurance, so we got him a nurse at my house until he had to go to assisted living. My neighbor the OG Perp died, and her grandkids moved in. It was downhill from there. With the same loud knock as years before like their grandad at my door one day. They advised me that they can smell cannabis and prefer we do not smoke near their house. They thought the AC condenser on their home sucked air in. We thanked them and they left.

They came back a second time this time it was the grandson who just lost his job earlier as we saw him bring a box of his office stuff home. He told me he knew all about my health issue but wants the cannabis smoke to stop. He had me in tears so another person in my home shut the door in his face, he had my dog upset too ranting on. That night their car alarm went off at 3:30 AM. They did that for months. We got cameras and recorded it and them.

The grandson likes to look in our windows and got into it with someone in my home because he was out of work and pestering us. He had jail tattoos and wore boxers he was very ugly inside and out. They had two babies using the medi-cal system for free, yet the dad was rich and bragged about using social services for his kids. The entire family was doing skits outside too and making me stressed out as my office and desk was at the front window so I can watch them.

Dad Perp would get drunk to deal with his mom the OG Perp, so he drove drunk while festering over cannabis. The telepathy would pretend to be them to make it worse. It was hard to figure it out at first. I decided not to worry what people say outside it is not my business and I moved on. Being sober and helping my dad were my two efforts, while researching targeting. The only two people I knew back in 2003 were Raven1 and Cheryl Welsh from emails only, so my research was not often.

We stopped buying cannabis from dealers and went to approved licensed cannabis shops, the street drugs are not safe. It kept me from using hard drugs and is my step-down medicine. I do not consider it a drug. The AA guy magically got money to buy a crappy house down the street. He may have sold me for a grant at the DA's office, which was common at that point because of new federal funds available during the dot-com downturn post September 11th, 2001.

AA guy had a severe bloated belly and needed a liver, he finally died. One armed bandit was at his funeral and ignored me. AA guys dog hated him and loved us, and we fixed her fur problem and baby sat her. AA guys wife would pop pain meds and pass out on the toilet, I had to save her one time and crawl through the window. She moved away after AA guy passed. AA guy would harass the dog club at the school and his neighbor who drank. The Perps Next Door called the police on us after a small discussion through our window and now festered on our home restoration. Thank goodness the 3:30 AM alarm stopped after the police threatened them.

The keystone cops stopped but the Perps next door kept on, so we named them the Pot-Nazis.

THE GREAT ESCAPE TO FREEDOM

As a kid I was lucky to have good neighbors on the other side of our house. Old man Vic would take me on camping trips, and I got hooked on the camper lifestyle. He had a lovely land spot near Clearlake, CA. I dreamt of that for decades at work and decided to go for it when I got older. He was a decent man and when he passed, we bought his car, a mint thunderbird.

I needed sleep and that alarm next door tortured me. I started getting my home ready for sale and went off on many trips in many locations in California to see if my telepathy would stop and to get a good night's rest. The only time it was better was at Mt. Madonna RV Park. That is located high in the hills of Santa Cruz, CA.

The neighbors had no idea if we were home or in our RV so we would see them on the home cam doing their routines, which I took to court later. They found the cameras and pointed and walked back in the house. We bought a new 2011 Winnebago 31-foot Class A RV and it was fabulous. Our two dalmatians Missy and Bubba came with us.

When I came home, I parked out front, so I got a couple tickets for parking on the curb which I did to let the folks across the street see traffic and keep my RV off the narrow street. I had to rent a storage spot for my RV down the street to comply. I only stayed overnight at my home, but it was verboten to the Perps Next Door.

When we put the house up for sale, the entire Perp Next Door family did a walk- through of my house during an open house, the realtor asked them to leave they were looking in closets and drawers. I had never planned on selling my house that early, but I took the loss.

I was now free and bought a simple home miles away to get away from that hell hole city. That house was too ghetto, so we sold it and moved far away, mostly to save money as the bay area was overpriced back then as it is now. We found a lovely home and moved in and sold the Winnebago. We got a budget RV and continued to travel locally.

PERPS TAKE ME TO COURT

I needed to keep my medical connections near my old home until I found a new set of doctors, I travelled back and decided to visit my old home after 3 years. Sitting in my new car eating a sandwich due to hunger- I see the Pot-Nazi Female come towards my car which is not near her home at all. She sniffs in my car for cannabis, and I tell her to go away she starts smart mouthing me and sets me off. I told her she was vexatious and litigious.

New Year's holiday we get a knock saying we have a package at 8 pm, it was a process server we tormented for hours until 4am where he broke and left. How did they find me, I used a PO Box and other measures to not be found? The papers were shoved into the mailbox and not served properly. Pot Nazi's dad works for lawyers doing filing and such so they had a legal hookup. We had 5 days to find a lawyer as it took them many days to find us already.

The lawyers we found were young cool and eager, they took our case and took my 2,500 cash, a bargain for a million-dollar civil trial, yes, she wanted one million dollars to buy a new house and change her families' names. She knew I had sold a house and want the rest of my cash. They still have no jobs. I only had 3,000 remaining in savings. We had DVDs of my video feeds of the Pot-Nazis acting up and running the car alarm at night and other times.

We wrote an honest narrative and off we went to the races. Court room smelled, the hallways smelled, it was horrible, and the Pot-Nazis showed up late. The lawyer they hired had bed head and was half asleep and was being verbally abused by the Pot-Nazis in the hallway. We had to move seats in the hall during negotiations because the plaintiffs were giving us dirty looks and throwing fits. We won and they got no money. They had to sign a mediation agreement to stay away from me and me from them for 3 years.

She ran out of the court room, down the halls outside screaming and running like a famous cartoon person who got caught in the dirty movie theatre. Never saw or heard from her until a few weeks later when the horn honking campaign started in front my new house. The house also got too expensive to own because of all the money we laid out on living, hiding and legal fees. So, we sold it, and moved into our RV.

We share expenses with our family member and decided to go full time RVing. My blood pressure and lifestyle improved when I because a nomad. No overhead hardly and you can move if you do not like someone next door. We have had issues with bad campers, and they usually get addressed by the staff at our locations.

GOING OFF GRID LITE

Let's face it, technology today allows you to be mobile and still be connected, so it can be feasible to go off grid lite and still have vital services you need to survive today. This Epub book can be read without stepping foot into a library. RV's can go boon docking without shore power or water for a couple weeks.

I operate my conference call in my RV using 20MBPS service, you do not need many services as the cell phone can be used for most. Many people in my life have loved my idea of perma-camping or glam-camping. You'll need handyman skills for an RV or have the cash to pay for repairs on the road.

The telepathy is still the same no matter where I go, but the ability to relax and read books while grounding/earthing help a lot. It was never my neighbors, as they had their own game in the hood. Airstream all aluminum campers provide little relief as this is a multi-trillion-dollar program, which I got caught up in from a shady DA guy next door.

Of all the wars next door I can finally control who is next to me. With all the craziness we see today, many campers leave often so you do not even need to move. Make sure you research your locations before you move there. Consider camping with a friend so you are not alone and have a witness.

Thank you for reading my book. You can find out more information on my website www.targetedwest.com . We have a book club and conference call. Always try to de-escalate as your neighbors know where live. Feel free to contact me via email. This is my first book.

BOOK TWO OF THREE

MY SYNTHETIC DREAM BOOK

TARGETEDWEST EPUB 2022©

Dedicated to every targeted person in the world

TABLE OF CONTENTS

THE BEGINNING DREAMSCAPE

This book is about synthetic dreams that are not normal to you and seem manipulated via 4th industrial revolution technology not known to the public. Little is mentioned of this technology for a reason, it can create false memories that cause you to think twice. Dreams are very powerful to many- they can steer someone to make a choice based on false brain data. It can cause someone to accuse someone of many things and cause riff in the family dynamic, which is engineered.

These are weaponized dreams, to cause the enemy to weaken over time, a perfect anti-personnel method to drive someone crazy by featuring traumatic memories they extract from your brain's memory. I feel it is part of the human brain genome project. The dreams cause a reduction in deep REM sleep by design to weaken you over time. Some Targeted Individuals report manipulated dreams yet have no synthetic telepathy. In my case, I get both. This book will go into detail on how this hideous technology needs to be defeated and educates you on how to tell if your dreams are real or fake. Lucid dreams like a cheap movie.

When you report these nightmares, doctors usually associate it with trauma. They are correct- it is trauma based but mind control in the form of a dream. When you share to a layman non-TI, they say of it is just a dream. Indigenous people trust in dreams and have a high regard for the message's dreams give. You could displace groups of people to other lands by hacking their dream experiences.

A famous cult movie describes a moment when one of the characters had a vivid dream about a war memory. We will get into that more later. TI's have told me on the TW conference call about their dream experience, so this is not uncommon. Literally every part of your body and its function can be hacked using remote technology, and they did not miss out on the power of dream manipulation.

They the powers that be claim these technologies are non-lethal. Driving sleep deprived to work a crappy job you settled for after your initial targeting is lethal. My synthetic telepathy asks me how the movies at night are during a bathroom break and I tell them they are lousy B-Movies at best. These brain movies include sex and violence, just like mainstream TV shows.

Dreams are personalized based on your own brain data. Based on familiar things and people like a custom suit fits perfectly to your body, this is plausible deniability being used in your dreamscape.

This is part of a system of total political and social control, and a form of slow kill remote eugenics by sleep depriving someone and creating negative memories can cause permanent damage to the brain and organs, as designed. Here is a link that describes what happens when someone does not get restful sleep:

https://en.wikipedia.org/wiki/Sleep_deprivation

This is very common in military and intelligence operations during interrogations, by playing loud music to keep the person of interest off their game. In my first book The Cold War Next Door my neighbors the Pot-Nazis set their car alarm off at exactly 3:30AM which according to the Internet is when someone can have a heart attack over shock, how did they know that, are they sociopaths for that method, I think so. I would get so mad I couldn't go back to sleep, and it ruined my day.

Have you had a dream you cannot forget? These false dreams create false memories that are very hard for the average person to decipher, my dreams started in 2015 when I moved to the Central Valley from the Bay Area to save money and find quiet. They stick in my head because they are basically like my telepathy- a preset skit that repeats the same scenes. They focus on my parent's house mostly, others I spoke to said they focused on their childhood home or base home they lived the longest in as well.

Weaponizing dreams are one of the many ways the 4th industrial military intelligence state and non-state actors control a subject these days. It is clean and leaves no trace or trail. Like I've said there seems to be a deliberate campaign to keep this dream data offline and out of books. I am going to try to change that with this prose and effort with conference calls, videos plus twitter and now this quick read. The hidden hand will not stop me.

If they have proven to manipulate dreams at MIT, then you know the black ops systems are decades ahead. Here is the link that talks about controlling a dream in the lab:

https://www.livescience.com/dream-manipulation-machine.html

So, the dreamscape is more widespread and creeping into neural brain science and more, to manipulate the subject so they act on those false dreams they the scientists have inserted into victims' brains. So, the victim accuses a family member of molestation or more. They tried to make my super solid stoic dad into a pedophile chasing me around the family home they fester on when I was a kid in one fake dream. It never happened.

Chinese have documented what the top dreams are people have, and some of my dreams match that study very closely. The synthetic dreams are probably deigned to mimic organic dreams so nobody can discover this secret technology. Family homes are one of the most common dreams they say. Most of my dreams are based on my home I grew up in, which is interesting to me.

My computer locked up now and I had to reboot, the document was saved by me in more than one place, so I recovered it, so I can continue. I am a retired tech worker and rarely have issues with this software. Others who have reported synthetic telepathy/dreams get the same interruptions when disclosing.

Do people share dream stories to you that are normal when you could never share the sadistic dreams you get nightly? Of course not, these dreams are so insane they defy reality, as designed to discredit you or make you seem mentally ill to others. People pay others to explain what the dreams mean to that client to get them to come back for more sessions and never cure or give comfort to the sufferer.

So many songs are about dreaming- the most natural method of refreshing your body and getting on with the day, but you cannot do that because you're suffering from sleep deprivation. I must sleep 12 hours to get 8, which is a terrible waste of my senior years.

MANIPULATED DREAM HISTORY

There is little history of dream manipulation on the Internet that I can find as of writing this book. The only one of few links I have found was shocking and mentions synthetic dreams. Here is one link that describes dreams manipulated by geomagnetic fields:

https://pubmed.ncbi.nlm.nih.gov/9347546/

So why is the military giving me fake dreams- are they using geomagnetic based cloned frequencies? The fact I get these fake dreams maybe is because I wrote C/O on my draft card in 1978 which started this whole covert harassment campaign on me 2 years later and is continuing today. That doesn't mean the DOD is involved, it is just their technology used on me. Most likely a contractor as there were many in Silly-Con where I grew up. Most folks locally did not know the big MIC operations in their own backyards in Santa Clara Valley.

The book The Manchurian Candidate mentions a manipulated dream about Chinese and Russian military generals. The main character gets angry when the other ex-military buddy can describe the dream in detail. According to folklore, Chinese have been able to manipulate dreams for centuries, but I doubt they are in my head making these lousy B Movies.

These are lucid dreams that put you in as first player. I believe they monitor your reaction to gauge brain spikes and other brain data for money and grants. They bring up dead people in my life past to see how I react. Sometimes I wake up sobbing because they distort everything in the controlled dream.

Such a secret weapon that is hidden in plain sight in very few locations on the Internet. There must be a reason for this as it is obviously powerful enough for me to write a book about it, and having you read it because you too are getting these hideous dreams from hell or are very concerned that may happen in your household one day.

I wonder how long this has been going on in the United States and why. Can it be done remotely from another country, as there are no firewalls or barriers for anyone to access other countries citizens. I am almost certain this is part of a suite of technologies many countries use to control people. It is a race to the top to whomever masters the minds of the world. It is a war weapons race.

These dreams are most likely as I've said part of a brain genome project and part of advanced silent weapons for quiet wars. It is a weapon of mass distraction like synthetic telepathy. Indigenous people flee their land to follow dreams inserted to gain access to develop land for industry, so it is more than distraction, it is destruction of the brain using a mind dream virus per Dr. Robert Duncan.

It is possible to have normal organic dreams, but how do you know if they the real deal? Took me a while to learn how to spot a false memory. Enjoy the good dreams you have and consider starting a dream diary to document the good and bad. I started writing down my synthetic telepathy/dreams in 2003 and plan on sharing my diary one day in another book.

FALSE MEMORY CREATION

Courts make you swear on a bible that your memory recollection, is pure and true so can you imagine how many court testimonies were created by dream manipulation. You know damn well many people went to prison by false memories of witnesses. Many business and personal relationships ruined by false memory too.

Dreams form in the temporal lobe of the brain. This region also creates and recreates memories. Someone has learned how to electronically influence that section of your brain to control society and you. I have been told dreams are uploaded using blue lasers during the daytime. That has not been verified but sure sounds plausible.

Families broken up over accusations that end up involving child protective services most situations having bad endings because of its obvious chaos and disarray at the services offices The book Legally Kidnapped describes the power of CPS. Once they get that bug in their head in any social service, the wheels of **bureaucracy start rolling it is difficult to undo any red flagged reports by social workers.**

Financial ruin by following a dream that was never going to pan out is an effective way to quell the enemy, as this is a war weapon by design. The Art of War mentions that making the enemy overspend and overreach ends up making them lose the conflict. So, who is behind this technology, shall we try to muse more about it, read on?

Indigenous people will act on dreams if that is normal for their local culture. One of my dreams is about fish, and indigenous people close to the land dream of fish and other animals which can be an omen to them, check this link out:

https://indigenousnh.com/2019/01/25/indigenous-dreams/

Like many native land people being cheated out of their lives living by scaring them away from their known land may be done electronically to gain control of the property all over the world. If you have these fake dreams, how do you cope and differentiate the differences between organic dream and manipulated. Feel free to drop by our conferences and share your story.

Have you acted on a dream? We have purchased a house based on one and it ended up being very lucrative- we were able to recondition the house and sell the investment for a tidy profit. Some of our dreams have not been very successful, my household knows the secret **magick** tricks being done to us. Keep your spirituality close by at all times.

Trauma can have an impact on a person's memory and traumatic memory can affect not only the brain, but also the body and nervous system as well. Loss of memory is a natural survival skill and defense mechanism humans have developed to protect themselves from mental damage from trauma. The military knows this and so do others and keep it hidden very well.

Organized crime or the syndicate is involved and may be using this to manipulate human trafficked people, so they will not tell someone or the authorities what happened or locations/people by replacing bad memories with good. Remote dream manipulation is a remote form of human exploitation, in a covert manner. My speculation is that some governments and organized crime work together in this program.

For fun here is a link showing how many songs have the word dreaming in them. Music, movies and media have an influence on people and that word is rather common because it is a big deal to people all over the world. Talking about dreams is always a fun parlor trick with friends unless you get military grade synthetic dreams. There is a band called Synthetic Dreams too just to make things more confusing, here is the dreaming stats link:

https://www.lyrics.com/lyrics/dreaming

I wonder if animals have synthetic dreams to make them attack their owner or run off and starve which hurts the indigenous people who depend on the lands to live off. I used to see my dog have dreams and wonder since he bit part of my nose off one day, that is another entire story. Giving animals trauma dreams may confuse them too.

We are going to the next chapter and describe the dreams in my household. I have cleaned most of it up because it involves drugs and sex. I do not do drugs and way too old for anything else.

They started the Rolex watch influencing around 1986 and hypnotized me to go buy a white gold trimmed stainless steel datejust on credit. I paid on it and paid on it. I had to file bankruptcy in 1994 because of it. I did not make the type of income for that level of watch, not even used.

It was remote weaponized financial demise, used in war to weaken the enemy. I was so cash poor I had to trade it for a transmission replacement, due to my car I could not afford being repossessed, another remote influenced purchase is to buy big ticket items on credit, with unaffordable payments.

They make me dream of buying cars often. I use wise advice from a man who lived to 112 years old. Pay cash-No credit. Sold my house and moved into an RV and loving it was my best idea of keeping it simple.

People dream of tiny homes and RV is a tiny home. The fake dreams still make it our here in the country at my peaceful farmland location where I can concentrate on exposing this hideous dream invasion technology with my prose.

I have never had a cannabis dream; it is always powder. Fake dreams of me hiding in bathrooms at work or anywhere consuming drugs, which I do not do. The chem-sex movies are very common every night. I am always coming down at my parents' house.

They have inserted my two aunts often in these dream-movies. I worked with my aunt at my fathers business and that is a common scene. She hates me and wont talk, that is untrue, she never stopped talking and loved me. Reframing old relationships is one of the top themes they offer to me at night.

The Rolex in my dreams falls apart often, last night I went to jeweler in my dream to have it fixed. I told him I had 3 Rolex, one was plastic and fell apart. I owe my drug dealer money since he fronts me the powder.

So, I had to give him one of my Rolex. I show my Rolex to many people pushing it into people's faces. Then it falls apart and they laugh. They have me dream buy cars that I never pay for, and they get repo 'ed at my parents' house. Even motorcycles I own in these silly dreams never got a payment.

One frequent dream is I end up at a rich friend's house, he lives in the Log Gatos hills. I hang out there often swim in their pool stay in one room and wander around high. I change clothes often, something I used to do high. I look way better and younger than my senior self, an evil way to give me flattery to get me to watch by force.

These are examples of forced false memories as I sometimes think it is true. I am quite sure a layman like me doesn't understand how these fake dreams cause permanent damage subconsciously in the brain deep somewhere. Could be the start of dementia to force false memory on the elderly who are lonely and gullible like me.

False and erased memory are tools of the military to protect national security for any country. This is world-wide, not just the USA.

I have no idea how technology works to do this, but I bet someone is selling it as a war weapon. It is cunning and can discredit someone or cause them to act on these memories. The same part of the brain does memory and the fake dreams as I mentioned earlier in the book.

Do you have a synthetic dream story? Send me your information, as this book is virtual and can be added to. If you want to make your own testimony book, we can show you how via email. The power of word in a book are profound.

www.targetedwest.com click on contact to send me a message. Link off for hard copy.

Now for more of my personal dreams. You may see a pattern from your own dreams in mine-read on.

MY SYNTHETIC DREAMS

Like I said earlier in the book, I started getting these dreams 15 years into my overt targeting that includes synthetic telepathy and directed energy towards my privates. The fake lucid dreams started at the same time as my CIA sex bomb effects. I moved away from the Bay Area and now my targeting got worse by adding these hideous dreams.

Hotels are common, and I am always on the move. I do drugs in the rooms often in the dreams and the baggy of drugs is always the same.

They have me going to my old drug connection my childhood friend who was down the street from my childhood home. I drive various cars I keep buying or ride bikes and scooters. Sometimes I have a motorcycle. I have been clean for two decades and this drug dream topic is a way for me to relapse by dreaming of drugs.

I had never worked out my mental health issues back then and resorted to street drugs to quell my confused and sick mind. The telepathy and the helicopter above my home in 2002 cleaned me up and made me perma-sober, I think they gave me the message to quit by accident.

I have a very good Doctor who I have on my speed dial in case I ever have any issues with drugs or needing to talk about these dreams. I have never told her my dreams are synthetic, I already share my synthetic telepathy opinions with her often.

They make me dream of cars I used to own. Their favorite is a 1981 Alfa Romeo Spider Veloce. It either gets stolen or I cannot find it in a shopping center parking lot. Sometimes parts get taken off the car in my dreamscape of lies. One time they made my car into a monster that chased me into the hills. It was a lucid dream as I was hiding behind trees from a car. Even the Italian painted bronzo metalico finish was spot on in color. They have me worry that I did not call the police to make a stolen car report and forget to call my insurance, which is silly. It shows up in my parent's garage and disappears in some dreams. I am a car hobbyist, and they play on that theme often.

Another car I owned and loved was a 1979 Dodge Magnum same as the Chrysler Cordoba but sportier. They had that car chase me into my neighbor's garage and I had to hide all night as it would come alive and run fast through a realistic neighborhood. Sometimes I drive it to a location to downtown San Jose, and I forgot where I left it and stress out over the car all night.

All my cars including my father's huge green Chrysler always show up as regular automobile in my custom dream. They show up in my dad's garage sometime all of them in smaller scale. All cars come alive in the garage and chase me into the house.

My friend the car dealer sold me cars often. Most were nice and some were crap. They always have him in my dreams selling me a junk car for 100 dollars a month. Like the first automobile membership club where I can change out cars at will.

Car dealer dude follows me all over for his payment in my phony dreams. He gets mad and scares me if I don't have cash. His personality was not that way, he was rather mellow. I sleep in the vans he sells me on The El Camino I cruised my hobby car at which never happened I never slept there.

None of the cars have current registration and I am scared to drive them. Most have no plates. The wheels get loose the cars float badly and it is hard to control these dream cars on the road.

They have me in the hills sometimes getting lost and fall into the Hetch Hetchy water system, a reoccurring theme. One time I had a huge Lincoln got a flat and the car place had it 100 feet in the air and the wheels fell off and I ran. Many road surfaces, roads of brick and dirt too.

I used to drive around a lot when I was a kid, so they chose this theme of me driving young to discredit my dream testimony. Driving through fancy neighborhoods with dead ends and neighbors watching me to make sure I drive slowly. Cars morph into scooters and motorcycles sometimes during my dream trek.

Sometimes they have me remotely driving the cars using line of sight which I lose and worry about. Sometimes I am in the passenger side driving. Night driving down a street by my home is common. Issues with the headlights happen often so I dream wreck.

Often, I am going the speed of light at high speeds, which I've never done, I was a fast driver as a kid but not going light speed. Interesting is they only feature three of my own cars I owned between the late 1970's and early 1980's. All other cars I dream of are from the rent a car dealer dude.

They have my father coming home with wrecks too he has a secret dealer he goes to also. Sometimes I need to go to work, and all the cars are gone, and I panic. Many of my work dreams are from a tech company I worked for, and so the drive is long, and I need a car with gas. My mother never drove and is not shown driving ever.

They have me at an amusement park in that far away city that is not far away due to gaffs in the process of making these synthetic dreams. It is mostly advanced artificial life more powerful than AI; it is your twin.

Quik Tech Talk: I speculate that the hardware for this is Advanced Quantum Machines able to render custom videos in seconds. Something that took days to do for one scene in hollyweirds graphic arts movie machine maker Silicon Graphics aka SGI in the 90's here is an older SGI machine:

Your brain data has been mostly captured to make these brain movies and new ones made on the fly using very powerful new quantum machines. Here is a picture of a D:Wave quantum machine server farm quite a size difference as you can see in the picture:

Now back to my personal dream testimony in that mystery city….

Now to the shopping malls and an old dance club I worked at. Nonstop dreams about walking in shopping malls and getting lost or losing my car and having to walk home. Many walks home dreaming. My friend who passed works at a café and I visit him sometimes at the shopping mall.

There is a secret city not far away but seems thousands of miles apart is a constant. Drug dealer and Car dealer and I drive there in the car guys new BMW 5 series. Even the orange glow of the dash is perfect. Car guy did own a pristine BMW coupe once, but this car is different, it is his work car the wholesaler he works at gives him to drive around in the pretend dreams.

The big club I worked at as the head DJ is always in my dreams. The owner visits with me and has a drink and does paperwork, he never did paperwork the manager did. The evil DJ who hated me in real life is in the dream often too. He harassed me in 2016 on Facebook in a DJ forum. Some people cannot let go.

I worry I am going to get drunk during the dream and drink light. The bar is like the TV show cheers it is in the basement in downtown San Jose, CA. The real club was on the corner off Julian Street, not in a basement. Because they cannot get faces and locations correct, everything in these shoddy movies is off by a long shot. Sizes and shapes are not even close.

A popular hotdog fast food place is featured often in my dreams, as I am often trying to get to the restaurant before they close. Sometimes they drive-thru involves intricate track systems like a warehouse. They have me going to the car wash often too off El Camino Real in Santa Clara, CA.

I end up in restaurants with strangers and ordering food that never shows up. Most these places in my dreams are closing for the last time.

The main theme I've got out of these series of manipulated dreams is they have one message. They are relationships I've had with people and places and never had a good ending. They take my small failures and make them huge; they make people I knew hate me when I interact with them in these lucid dreams.

They fester over a 30-mile section of the main drag in town that leads towards San Francisco. I usually end up in Burlingame in downtown, which I travel to from Fremont, CA on my lunch hour from work. That company was very strange and had a secret owner. It is impossible have lunch that far away, because it involves a bridge. Another fatal flaw that is so obvious and poorly planned in this covert dream technology.

That company was the leader in data collection for the printing industry, maybe an early intel agency investment to monitor print shops is my guess. It is the only tech job of my many on my resume' that show up in my dreams. I do dream of other tech companies like the one down the street, I just walk in and start working while having my main job down the street.

I did have a dream I worked at apple, but they never gave me a cubical and I stood all day worrying I am going to get fired. The getting fired theme is very often. I've never been fired or laid off at any tech company. They have a scene where I never get my computer and phone to do tech support. I sit in rooms with others, and they all have monitors and phones and I sit there worrying and I complain to my old real boss who is now an evil devil lady and talks down to me.

We always had world class IT support for our workplace in tech. We always had phones and computers and cubicles empty and ready no matter where I worked. I remember after a layoff or a building move of a group seeing an ocean of blue colored cubicles.

They have me come to work shirtless and walk around shirtless all day-sometimes I come to work in my robe.

They have me failing in school in my dreams while ordering me to go back to school in my synthetic telepathy. When I last had schoolwork, I was verbally abused so bad I needed to play music loud to get through my courses at home. Took me three times to get my math exam correct. They seem to be anti-STEM and do not want people to succeed in science, technology, engineering and math.

Keeping society feeble is their goal, they do not want smart workers-they want obedient hard-working employees who ask no questions and are loyal to a fault. They like to have me walk out of classes every dream, the class is mostly younger people, not age coordinate for a typical school.

My cars never work or are missing when it is time for me to go to work in my dream. When my workday is over, I cannot find my car in the parking lot. I always park next to the door in real life. They have me driving around Fremont, CA in the hills getting lost while I should be at work. The hills are in the wrong place, the bay water is where the hills are, so they are way off again.

The current theme as of this writing is how I get fired and still come to work and do my job for free. They show my paycheck stubs and my bank accts being empty, my father getting worried I have no money. I am having troubles getting a new job which is poppycock, I had a professional tech recruiter on speed-dial in real life and never had an issue moving to other tech firms which is very commonplace in that industry.

The average time of employment at any firm for me was 4 years, usually a business cycle was causing the business to be stagnate and most tech workers know it's time to find the biggest newest hot tech and split the scene. Tech recruiters cold call too and fish talent quickly with little fanfare. It is obvious to you the reader that my dreams are a form of psychological operations being done to my memories.

Take someone's good life and make it into a satanic sadistic B Movie in their head, to reframe the good memories with bad. Could you imagine how this dream manipulation technology could help us with positive dreams by using cognitive behavior therapy and other methods to treat someone with a mental illness or add value to their life with good thoughts? They create mental illness and the hand that controls the world always has.

Resources for behavior health is very limited. It is not covered by most insurance and the meds they push are not always the best. You could create a Manchurian Candidate with this dream manipulation debauchery, and they know that and have discussed that in secret back rooms funded by dark money.

If you went to a dream specialist who decodes dreams for a living, they would never be able to know your dreams may not be your own thanks to 4th industrial revolution technology which is covert and hidden from the public.

We talk about our dreams on the conference calls often. They are usually trauma based and can cause others who hear it to get triggered. Most folks not targeted prefer not to hear our gory ugly fake dreams from hell, they will tune you out. It is designed that way.

They the dream masters want to rub the fact in this morning when I was sleeping about the reality that my father gave his rental property away because I had AIDS. Have HIV but he called it AIDS and he said I am going to die soon. He died 5 years ago, and I am still here idiot father.

My father's business partner gave his rentals to his son and they have me living in one of his units illegally, every night I worry I have to move out, they made me a squatter on his rentals. They have my mother on her sofa at our family home talking to me, it is so sweet to see my mother again.

They had a couple at my parent's home to buy it this morning, I could see the realtor and clients from down the street. I had a fancy new black car I sat in down the street. They like to stress you over your base locations.

Grind in the fact of your losses in life to create never ending PTSD and trauma over not having secure housing is one way to break down the enemy, me a tax paying legal human on this earth with no criminal record. They pick anyone for this never-ending dream experiment.

My second serious relationship is rekindled with dreams of this person being blind and sick and out all the time partying. So far from the truth. I live in his apartment too on top of other locations of insecure housing scenarios. He was in AA, so I come home drunk, which is not true. Brain data gleaned to be used as a weapon to break the war enemy down.

I was at work again at the Covalent, what a name huh? Very Covert, owned by secret people. My boss is featured again, I helped make a business deal and have checks to give her. She nods and thanks me, I remind her I am fired and need my job back. Focus on false failures to break my confidence down. I am retired and out of the work force, why rekindle old work memories? That is because overall this technology is flawed and not perfect. Where do they hide these devil machines and who works on them? Those are classified and the employees are compartmentalized to prevent leaks.

So, in closing you now know to not follow your dreams unless they are true to reality and your heart. This soulless machine from hell cannot replace our souls and natural life energy. You should have an idea how to spot them and jot a note down in your diary. Dollar stores has those small notebooks and pens. Grab some and have at it.

Thank you for reading my short story book. We can teach you how to make your own testimony book online. This is my second Epub book.

BOOK THREE OF THREE

MY SYNTHETIC TELEPATHY: TARGETED INDIVDUAL STORY

BY DJ CHRIS

2022 TARGETEDWEST EPUB

Dedicated to the targeted community who have supported me and purchased my writings. May this book help you understand your own situation with telepathy. I have talked to over one hundred people who have the same experience of telepathy, some call it V2K, some call it by other names. Either way you've got an unwanted conversation going on, I hope my story can help you find peace with this 4th industrial mess.

TABLE OF CONTENTS

CHAPTER ONE: THE FIRST YEAR IS ALWAYS THE WORSE

As I mentioned briefly before about my telepathy in my two published Epubs, this third book will go into more details about the conversation I have with the terrorists in my head, and let you decide for yourself, is it organic or electronic. People can have telepathy for many reasons even health conditions can cause hallucinations and to create havoc on someone's life including the family who loves them and is concerned and has no one to turn to for help at that moment.

Society freaks out when you admit you talk to someone in your head. They usually say oh dear that is your inner voice, but in my case it may not be. I learned so much from the telepathy and verified online what these brain bandits said to me and have documented it in my diaries I've kept since 2003. They call me a POS for over twenty years, and I still do not think that, as I have developed a natural brain aversion to block those words.

The first thing I heard via the mind hackers was a comment about me hiding in my hallway with my doors closed, I could tell I was being watched by my 6th sense and they said a derogatory comment about my sexuality not worth repeating.

"HEY WHY YOU IN THE HALLWAY?"

I am in the middle of a drug relapse and the drug seems to be a truth serum as I am interrogated in my bed for two days. It was a man and women and not any type of chatbot or AI talking. They asked me about my entire life and would ask me over and over the same questions for hours like a CIA agent would.

As I have mentioned before in my books and conference, I knew in 1974 that the brain can be hacked told to me by a friend I knew on the CB/HAM community. The brain has no firewall and uses frequency waves that can be captured.

He worked on the Telstar technology and that was his handle. He was a hippie that drove his family in an old VW bus and lived around the corner from me, so we could talk via the radio often, and meet up with others in parking lots mostly.

We used to follow the semi corrupt city police and monitor them in the late 1970's using CB radio and police scanners. They hated injustice and as a young man back then so did I, so it was a good friendship. He gave me career and education advice too which he directed me to be a tech worker.

So, I knew the telepathy interrogation game was not real and decided while high to make up stories to them. I could tell they had no access to how I felt or my basic body functions back then- all they had was my word which was gibberish.

The first course of business is to permanently sober up for life and not consume hard drugs and stick with cannabis. The sheriff helicopter was over my home recently and the interrogation sounded like them, very Law and Order so I knew I had a new enemy thanks to my neighbor the recovering alcoholic prosecutor for the county who was watching us.

The voices screamed not to go get help, but I did and asked the recovering attorney if he had some booklets on AA meetings, since AA did not have much of an internet presence in 2002.

Today they have AA and NA meetings online for help but are not a replacement but a good backup in my opinion. Be careful when you attend meetings not to give too much information out, I told them I was here to learn, and they left me alone. I have had both adverse and positive memories of the recovery community. Back to the fun part of telling you what they say.

They said they were looking for criminals and people who hurt kids, and I laughed because I told them they are the criminals.

My diary said they tried to pretend to be the neighbors behind my home, which is not true. Why would my neighbors the two old senior ladies be interrogating me, therefore you should know who lives near you- the telepathy skits will not work.

The first year is the worst as I said, and the telepathy would argue with itself and sound like a mad female and a male in authority. The female would talk to me through the window between 2-5 am when I used the bathroom. My diary in 2004 mentions how tired I was of them making comments about everything I do like the Truman show and I was tired of it.

During this time, I complained in my diary about depression and anxiety, was it technical or was it natural from hearing demonic voices that say rude comments constantly. I have since started taken anti-depressants to help my mood, they work for me but not for everyone, as they dull emotions and have side effects.

They were always telling me something bad is going to happen and back then I absorbed it and carried it in my thinking.

I trained myself not to take them seriously, ever. I do not negotiate with brain hacking terrorists. Much of what they say and tell me what to do is not congruent to my own personality profile which is why it is so easy to detect false NLP words and feelings of false emotion.

Neuro Linguistic Programming is one of their tools, which I knew nothing of back then when I had not had resources to research back in the beginning of the Internet.

The telepathy only knows what my brain knows and cannot tell me what is going on outside of my world. In one of my diaries later I meet people with the same words they hear and behavior of these mind hackers. I started meeting others who had the same beginning story too of my targeting. Always starts with the local authorities, even if you have a clean record.

They tell me I am going to a nursing home often, so they can do experiments on me, even when I was in my early 40's they said the nursing home comment.

They are very law and order and are looking for crimes, they tell me they get a reward if they catch anyone. Later I found out just the targeting is how they make money and doing human trafficking by broadcasting us to customers too eager to see some victim thru their mind by a hacking method, they want the latest technology and are usually very wealthy.

The questioning never ends in my head, they are the same for others. It is a form of psychic driving by remote methods for many and involve personal information they gleaned during the interrogation process at the beginning of my overt targeting.

CHAPTER TWO: SHOCKING FIND- INFORMATION ONLINE

Thanks to people like Raven1 and Heart who put together early targeting sites like MindControlForums.Com and others I was able to get over the first year of a CIA style takedown in my head, loss of sleep and no energy were my symptoms too.

March 23rd, 2004, I mention in my diary that the voices tell me they are the illuminati, which I knew nothing about at all or even spoke that word. Anyone can call themselves whatever they want, and telepathy is no exception. But the research led me to my father the master mason, as it was his home I was in when first contacted via telepathy.

I ask the telepathy why me and they never answer. They tell me it has nothing to do with myself and is an experiment on many.

They are offering me $75.00 per hour to work for them and stop this book as I type. I have told them I have no interest in their lucifer light bringing to my life or money.

Many new jobs for defense contracting involves words that describe this technology and brain law enforcement of thoughts, it is out in the open.

Kindle got popular for TI's who have trouble publishing their stories of targeting, and I found several books on the subject by Dr. John Hall and Dr. Robert Duncan which you could never find in a regular library back in the mid 2010's.

I decided to go back to school, and the telepathy made it close to impossible to study at home. That is when I learned a portable radio works great and got me through my work.

Before you go and run out and buy a radio, remember it did not work for my friend, it distorted the music.

They tell me I am going to be put to sleep, which is not true I am still here as I type. Going on-line showed me examples of others getting death threats from the brain invaders.

There were no published conferences to go to for help, I had no phone lifelines with any TI, I was alone and decided to tell my doctor which had good and bad outcomes.

I told my immune system doctor, and he wouldn't listen, acted hinkey as hell and referred me to a psychiatrist, who turned out to be very helpful as I still see her as of today with great results.

My telepathy mentions the HIV doctor often, but never mentions my shrink, very odd.

CHAPER THREE: MEDICATION MADNESS DISCOVERY CIRCUS

My first visit my doctor suggested medication as that is her specialty, she is a pharmacologist, and I knew that coming into the relationship. I told her from the beginning half of me thinks it is organic the other thinks it is technology.

First, we tried Seroquel and Buspar, both made me a zombie and I was unable to function. I gave the medication plenty of time and was supervised by my new doctor-feel-good.

The voices laughed and never got quiet, the medication did not make them go away, matter of fact I lost my natural immunity and health to ignore them, as a lifeless bed ridden fool, they got worse.

Voices now pretend to be a loved one who died of AIDS to break me down. They doubled their effort to break my soul.

The dreams I wrote about back then coincided with the telepathy. The doctor increased the Seroquel, and the voices did not go away. They talked as if they used the neighbors direct-tv dish to talk to me while in the bathroom their favorite room to harass me, as it is private time for humans.

After telling doctor-feel-good I needed something for anxiety she got me hooked up on Ativan. It made me angry and did not help me at all. It took me a year to get off the medication and on Christmas of that year I gave myself the gift of no benzos no more.

The pharmacies acted unprofessionally when they filled my Ativan script because it was a class 3 drug, so I also quit the medication because of the hassle.

At the same time a person who worked for me when I was a supervisor for a tech companies technical support department was calling. He called from 12:00 midnight till the morning, and kept asking me if I was ok, I told him I'm getting a restraining order and hung up, He claims he worked for the CIA before and has a movie script he wrote.

I am sure he has nothing to do with this harassment, but I would easily flip out at anyone who acted suspicious the second year of my targeting-telepathy symptoms.

The telepathy took that phone call and tortured me with false skits to make me think my ex-coworker was in on it.

One entry into my medicine trial period said the medicine made me less scared of the voices in my head. I finally found two medications that helped me with my depression and helped me sleep. The problem is the Risperdal made me gain 60 pounds and I now have managed to rid myself of 20 so far and made me fat my worst fear, since I was self-aware of my looks and wanted to be healthy.

I have tried to get off that drug, but the side effects are crazy and debilitating. I will try again one day when I have the mental strength to handle that withdraw. I may need to seek medical help to get me off that drug. It also lessens your life span.

My diary muses about me opening my third eye, and I have never discounted that as a possibility I am talking to entities in the 4th dimension.

By this time the voices were winning, and I was giving up. I was talking to them and having a conversation which was new. They were judgmental and sounded like the authorities still. Still having horrible dreams at the same time, meaning my torture was 24/7/365 even on holidays.

My HIV doctor seemed concerned and did an MRI it showed nothing and was my baseline I can use today if I get another MRI or imaging of my head.

The Risperdal caused gynecomastia and my male breasts got bigger and sore and painful, it deformed my body to this day just to make some telepathy go away. It did not work they made comments on all the medical work we did.

Every time I told my doctor it was the medication, she told me it was the cannabis doing it. She said it was white bread and sugar making me fat not the medication.

I practiced moderation on everything with no help. At one time I weighed 368 pounds. I am now 315.

Part of that weight gain was from having sugar at night and not getting out and moving or working out walking or walking my dog Mojo, a very regal Dalmatian who loved us dearly, he finally got me out and about and we joined a dog owners club nearby.

The voices followed me into the backyard, and I would stare at my neighbor's fence thinking it was them. They were druggies who had not sobered up and used to stay up all night waking me up when I did get sleep.

My diary mentions the sexual dysfunction I was getting from the medications I was trying to stop the telepathy; it was soul breaking; it almost broke me, and my diary said I wanted to give up, but I did not.

CHAPTER FOUR: SEND IN THE NARROW AI NLP CHATBOTS

The blowback from the new post September 11th remote torture was strong and fierce. I was fighting back with humans through a technology, and I was breaking them, they were quitting after I would turn the tables on them and gave them exactly what they gave me, misery.

Supervisors would come on and tell me I was hurting their employees and that they were very concerned. This is when the narrow AI chatbots started filling in space between conversations. It was pure CIA psychic driving in a form of a repeating loop.

The human agents would mimic the chatbot so they blended in, but I could tell by their one fatal flaw. The AI doesn't use my name, the humans do because they are looking at a screen for their orders. They told me each agent gets 60 people per day to talk to.

The first language bots or chatterbots sounded like a grindy robot machine with dry gears. It somehow modified my brain to listen to them over time, so they had a normal voice tone after a few weeks.

The telepathy took a new turn of mostly repeating the same words and phrases over and over. Many words had double meaning, and some had hidden meanings I still to this day cannot decipher.

My left eye went crooked during this time, I have seen many people who are famous with crooked eyes who I know are illuminated. Did I become a project for the luciferians my dad hung out with? I am not famous, but I feel I have been lit up.

So many physical changes due to medication and the program I got put into by who knows, now my eye looks terrible. The telepathy makes fun of that.

The chatterbots have been the main player and I noticed they slowed down and put me in maintenance mode as they said. They were getting nowhere with me and were frustrated.

People can be tricked by chatterbots in dating and texting on a phone, and think they are real. This is the same concept, but they speak out words and sound human, but lack emotion or inflections a human would have while speaking.

The other fatal flaw in their system is lack of continuity, the humans use way more words off the scripts while the language bot are limited in vocabulary.

My friend in the conference calls reminded me of archons, that could be the AI style chatterbot I was hearing, it is possible this could be off earth, as only an idiot would think we are the only intelligent species in this universe.

During holidays the chatterbot or called language bot turns to a live human agent. They told me they get paid for this as a second job and use their time off their main career to do this.

Some tell me they bought a franchise from a well-known defense contractor and are losing money and may lose their house. Karen Stewart hired a private investigator and he found this to be true, it is called the William Patrick Cox home franchise.

I assume the chatterbots were activated by hand but now use advanced super intelligence to track and control what they say. It is almost impossible to tell a human from a robot now, the technology has advanced to this day in 2022.

Many investments into quantum based super computers were happening and this was an easy trick for a machine of that high caliber to make telepathy and other biological effects. It was the beginning of the 4th industrial revolution of hacking the enemies' minds for a less lethal combat-less silent weapons; less lethal they say. They are slow kill machines with human operators along with automated chaos. They threaten the FBI on me often.

"THE FBI WATCHES YOU AND KNOWS EVERYTHING"

"THE POLICE WILL BE THERE AT 3:00 AM"

"WHAT WE HAVE HERE IS A LACK OF COMMUNICATION"

They mention famous people like Michael Jackson and Anderson Cooper. They like to announce that people died that I know or knew. They are obsessed with Sex and Death and Law and Order.

They make you have dark thoughts that any normal person like me would never do. Why would I take medications for my immune disorder to then off myself. I have no plans on leaving the earth for a couple more decades at least.

MIT is the source of chatterbots and may be the source of the technology, not saying they are using it on me, but they developed it.

I have limited the telepathy technology by turning off fans and anything with a motor. Why the bathroom gets hit the most, because we use a fan when we visit it. They create a vortex according to a known moderator.

The chatterbots and humans ask me if I want to go eat at a famous chain starts with Apple… They mention the famous taco place that has a "ring" to it. They mention banks too like the one you never leave home without. This is NeuroCommerce© that I have reported on my conference call shows on the TargetedWest study group on Sundays.

CHAPTER FIVE: SINGULARITY VIA ADVANCED INTELLIGENCE

Advanced quantum super computers now operate most of my targeting. It knows me very well as I am too much like a robot after being entrained by one for a few years and having a technology career background. Here is a little ditty from the director of technology at Google:

"By the time we get to the 2040s, we'll be able to multiply human intelligence a billionfold. That will be a profound change that's singular in nature. Computers are going to keep getting smaller and smaller. Ultimately, they will go inside our bodies and brains and make us healthier, make us smarter." Ray Kurzweil

That technology is here and used on me and others to convert decent humans into a transhuman who can take commands better from the neural network. They say DARPA and technologists of exotic technologies are decades ahead, this is testimony that it is real and current, not in 2040.

So, who are they? Most likely a defense contractor or scientist who is experimenting with MKULTRA 2, the technology sequel. Funded by governments throughout the world for behavior and political control of the masses. Psychiatrists invent new scripts based on CIA black site torture centers all over the world to try to break me and others. They have had two decades, and I am not broken.

The main reason is to find out if you are patriotic to your home country, they have been looking for communists for decades using drugs and torture and yet found none.

I am sure the advanced super intelligence is a product of the USA and is sold like other war weapons the banana republic is known for. The brain genome project is their way of mapping the human brain as they have with me. They find old memories and comment on them to see my reaction. They access short term memory to play skits in your head. Much of this is done using advanced super computers.

As of September 20th, 2022, the telepathy I have is now mostly AI based, no more human contact except when I act up. The machine listens to my conversations online and in person and comments, it is just another weak parlor game they think will trick me. This is that level of separation so they can blame the machine for the errors in judgement or blame a defense contractor for the mess they have created.

Humans are more resilient than they figured, the brain bounces back with its plasticity and can heal. Society may need more time as they are influencing people in mass levels, mind controlling people to buy and do things they do not feel comfortable doing, because it is a game. It is the Hyper Game and is used in military and business.

Occasionally I get a hive mind event where more than person is talking to another making observations about me, it may be the AI talking to each other or perpetrator agents making notes for their grand experiment.

Then they ask some of the dumbest questions all day long. They keep interrogating me but are having less to work with, as the other accusations have disappeared like the famous Law-and-Order crap. I am sure there are more than one agency involved, and that tone is most likely the DOJ or a contractor for them.

The machine does not like when I repeat it, it will go nuts. It takes much energy to do that.

I must wait until I am in a rancid mood to go after them. They like to ask me if I know who they are, I answer I do not care. They used to filter my words too to mask the city I lived in as if they are protecting something in Silicon Valley where I grew up.

The huge fatal flaw is after trillions of dollars in making this hideous mind control system is that it cannot detect lies. It can only read the subvocalizations you make when you talk back to them. They can retrieve a memory but cannot detect a fib. That is so pathetic and sad, it makes me laugh. It even follows a lie you say that had no common sense to it.

The machine can now inflict things like bowel movements or other biological effects. They can make you sneeze, cough and have other effects which make you a lousy war soldier. This is simply an expensive toy that causes discomfort for your enemy in war. It is a weapon of mass distraction that can make you fall and get hurt by having to be forced to talk to it when you are a senior like me.

I hope you research mind control and find out what I have discovered that man wants man to be connected to a computer using a BCI. Elon Musk is working on that now and his competitor is now using a real human to wire up thin copper threads into your brain that detect neurons firing that can be decoded by a chip implanted into the back of your neck.

Some jobs in the future may require you to be enhanced.

"BASIC INCOME FOR THE NON-CONNECTED"

The machine and sometimes a human agent chimes in when I chose my topics for the conference call. They scream and demand I do not talk about things like Masers, G.W.E.N. and how they use quantum entanglement remotely to connect to our DNA resonance- a very powerful signal our body resonates.

Quantum computers talk to our DNA and manipulate it in many ways, using scalar wave technology. They are screaming at me now to stop writing this book, which will not happen, I am micro focused on using books and social media plus conferences to spread the word about this evil technology.

Phased array antennas plus ground wave antennas and radar can be part of the source. They weaponize everything these days so they can control humans and make them obey.

Satellites monitor and track us using our bodies resonance. This is a multiprong multi-level multi agency and worldwide system. People who disclose it are called mentally unstable and locked up like the Soviet Union did to label dissidents. This is pure digital zersetzung. It must be stopped, and it can be done by spreading the word that invasive mind enslavement is a real thing.

My diary says, "why are they doing this to me?" and the telepathy answered, "because we can".

CHAPTER SIX: SHADOW OF ME – THE CLONE KNOWS IT ALL

Just when I thought I had mastered this technology they add a new feature, my clone. It is a copy like a presidential model Cathy O' Brien mentions in her book "TRANCE Formation" she mentioned she was trained to study and remember documents and recall them on demand as a president or dignitary asks for them verbally.

They will claim they can treat dementia and give vital information to the person needing help with language, yet use it was a war weapon. They will cause illnesses.

When this is public people can program the clone to assist in business giving someone an upper hand. Actors can teach the clone to repeat words for a movie or play so they can rehearse.

The hive mind system can be used in war with clones that can give the soldier uplifting messages and monitor their mental health based on their personal brain scan information stored on the cloud. They can use DARPA's ElectricRX to give the fighter remote treatment.

The war clone can remind the soldier of their stated mission and monitor him for any dissent. Lonely, the enlisted will talk to their clone and share their passions and fears during the conflict which will be recorded for reference.

"SEND IN THE CLONES, DON'T BOTHER THIER HERE"

So is my friendly clone helping me or hindering. My guess is hinder, as the good positive aspects of this brain technology will be shared and used by the wealthy and elite to stay above us, so they can look down at the human nodes.

My clone often asks me why I treat them poorly and fight back, he claims I am harassing them, and I am in their frequency, which is not true. They tuned into my resonance and are targeting me using advanced quantum based scalar waves.

He asks me when I am going to give up and I tell him I do not know how to give up. This is too interesting for me to ignore, the tech makes you answer the chatterbots, humans or the clone. Even the supercomputer complains that I am going to expose them.

They tell me I am the chosen one who will make this technology go away, the clone will go in rest state and come out in the next generation and relearn another human but this time they will have decades of experiments and discoveries to take this hideous technology to a new level, probably a fast kill option instead of the slow bake method of long exposure of radiation and microwaves.

When all else fails, the clone and chatterbots tell me I am going to prison. They cannot tell me why, but that is the blank threat I get when I push them too hard. Aren't I already in a floating box prison that follows me no matter where I go on this planet?

If this is mental illness, then why does the narrative in my head never change and why does it start at 8:00AM. Mental illness last time I checked was not based on a clock. Tried different activities- did not change nor waking up at different times it was right on time with the talking.

I discovered this was happening to others like my friend we will call "N" she has the exact same symptoms the skits the same, the on-time behavior of the tech is obvious to her too. Her clone and AI tell her it's Lawrence Livermore Labs doing this, which may or may not be true. They may have discovered the technology there, but a creepy well connected defense contractor or brain sciences doctor are probably our handlers.

Will they dream that our epigenetics will change to reflect this transhuman experiment, and then we become replicating well behaved Manchurian Candidates who follow commands and take orders with no errors. Will your futurist employer access your clone while you sleep to get updates on a project you are working on? Yes, he will and yes, they can.

Other than a human physical presence, you will have no value unless you are enhanced and that will be your total worth. Linked-In will have a section for enhanced humans and people will line up for blocks to get the BCI implant chip and be wired up for work.

Entrainment centers will flourish and have franchises so everyone can make money off this 4th industrial technology, that has been in the human's mind as a solution for over 100 years. A Technocrats wet dream will be real, and the stock market will reflect the human enhancement movement.

The only time I got relief was in the mountains of Santa Cruz, CA it was explained to me that I felt forest bathing and was on the back side of all the parabolic dishes pointing at the Santa Clara Valley. As I suspect, they use many methods to broadcast to me 24/7, many communications systems have the capability to do this and have been weaponized for social control and crowd management during possible future purges and I see the criminal unrest happening as we speak in 2022.

Yes, it is possible to create distress and havoc in a city for example, Prince the famous singer musician told us they would spray the skies with chemicals in the ghetto, then everyone would act up. This technology and a manipulating clone in me are a digital form of that, some will get enhanced and the ones they deem to be useless eaters will get the slow kill waves.

"ALL ANIMALS ARE EQUAL, BUT SOME ANIMALS ARE MORE EQUAL" *

*From the book Animal Farm by George Orwell which is not his real name, and he hangs with Huxley too, like predictive programing it seems they wrote about our current times.

It is 7:55 Am my clone will show up in 5 minutes and I must wake up at 5AM just to write this book. It is a sad game I play to try to win against these criminals, it is nonstop on-going and stressful. I think it is time for others to share their stories via a book or blog.

This is my third book and the powers that be in my head have made it almost impossible to do my work.

Even TargetedPerps© get involved to run me out of town. Spies for other conference calls and organizations email each other with fervor over everything the adverse TI says. Screaming at me when I share my work is not cool, telling me to f*** off is not very nice. This book would already be written but my last book "My Synthetic Dreams "was sidetracked and I was told not to promote it on other people channels.

So, I work alone and will always do that. By nature, I am a loner and isolation doesn't bother me, I use it productively to write my prose and blogs. If I hurt feelings, I am sorry but the non-telepathy folks out there need to understand this is not fun and games this is a slow kill death sentence being done to us targeted telepathy victims.

My clone wants me to go back to school, but I am a senior and cannot afford school debt and feel I will be indoctrinated to put things like He/Him on my Twitter profile and fuss for hours about non important civil rhetoric. My lack of education did not hinder me, I had a very successful tech career in Silly-Con Valley since 1980. My first job was drilling holes in circuit boards using an NC router. Very accurate work needing special skills including programming the NC router tape using X and Y location commands.

My passion has been and is music, I am a professional DJ since 1982, this is my 40th year working in night clubs and events in Bay Area. Now that I have slowed down, I put my mixes on mixcloud.com under mixtrax, you'll love the energy the mixes put out and it helps me do my upper body movements while I listen by moving to the beats.

The clone is here it is 8:14 AM. Make coffee and ignore him is my mantra. I suspect they will have physical presence machines with your clone and brain mapping memory installed after we are dead. You see the Illuminati-Entertainment complex using clones of Whitney Houston to perform her songs when she lived. People pay to see this.

Holographs of people is not my thing; I would rather watch/listen to her older works and movies and get my thrill of her talent. She was also targeted by the paparazzi in helicopters above her home for years. Thanks goodness music makes my telepathy go away, but I cannot play music 24/7 so they creep in and make their comments to break your natural entrainment for work and pleasure.

Now for the way I made this book.

This book is 1/3 of my total output in the literary arts, I have two others I will combine to make a paperback version called the "The Targeted Trilogy" which will include all three of my works.

If you would like to comment or make kind suggestions, please feel free to write to me at: djchris@targetedwest.com

I can advise you how to make a testimony book like this one via email, I do not do phone calls. Once you publish your works you will feel great. These books help meet expenses, I have been asset striped and live in a camper. I used to be a landlord and owned my own home but got run out of my town my neighbors and my father, he did not want no one owning no duplex's that can't work so he gave them to the handyman. My father did not understand the passive income method and the fact he ruined my retirement strategy so I will be working until I turn 80.

DJ Chris

United States Press Association Member

Thank you for purchasing my Targeted Trilogy book. Links are disabled obviously on the print book, epub version has links ☐